THIS COULD..."

How Two Words Create Opportunity, Increase Creativity, and Reduce Waste

By Scott Burnham

Print On Demand Edition

ISBN: 978-1-945971-09-9

For all correspondence: sb@scottburnham.com

CONTENTS

"There's music in all things, if men had ears."

Lord Byron

SECTION ONE

NEW NEEDS NEED NEW TECHNIQUES

Jackson Pollock was asked in an interview why he painted in a technique so different from the representational style of past artists, and in which he was formally trained. He explained that in an era of great change, "New needs need new techniques."

"The modern painter cannot express this age, the airplane, the atom bomb, the radio, in the old forms of the Renaissance or of any other past culture. Each age finds its own technique."[1]

Pollock was referring to artistic expression, but the core message is even more relevant today. In an era of unparalleled change and challenges in our resources and environment, we are still expressing ourselves in the old forms of consumption and consumerism.

The vast majority of us no longer create—we consume. We don't explore the future potential of the things we already have—we discard them and buy more. Decades of consumption have created a regrettable legacy for our time.

Researchers estimate that approximately half the iron, nickel, copper, and other base metals that have been extracted from the ground have been discarded or are no longer in use[2].

The amount of solid waste disposed of in the US has more than doubled in the last 50 years. In 2018 alone, more than 146 million tons of material solid waste were landfilled.[3]

Waste comes in many forms beyond discarded goods. Cities large and small are filled with objects, buildings, and infrastructure, built decades ago to serve people's needs—as their needs were, decades ago.

These are assets that should be reimagined for better contemporary use to meet the needs of growing and changing populations.

Our age will be defined by what we do with the resources we have, how we behave with our material assets going forward, and how we meet society's needs with existing assets, reduced budgets, and limited public funds.

Previous techniques got us into this situation—new techniques are needed to meet the new needs of the future.

The Coronavirus pandemic exposed the shortcomings of many systems and societies, revealing vast chasms between need and resources available to meet those needs.

Yet something else was revealed during the pandemic. For the first time in decades, resourcefulness became part of the collective consciousness as a means of getting through difficult times. An awareness of the benefits gained by doing more with what was already at hand came into focus.

As a post-pandemic recovery begins, we must not forget that needs will always occur more quickly than resources can be obtained or created—particularly now that the economic crisis has devastated public budgets.

The National League of Cities estimates that in the United States, cities, towns and villages can expect to face a $360 billion budget shortfall from 2020 through 2022.[4]

In July 2020, European Commission President Ursula von der Leyen said the EU budget for the next seven years would contain a number of "inadequacies" as funds were diverted to economic recovery packages. The bloc, said von der Leyen, faced "a very lean long-term EU budget," with funding reductions for research, health, and investment programs.[5]

I have spent decades working with cities, organizations, and individuals to do more with the resources they already have. Needs and priorities change with culture and country, but the fulcrum point for change remains the same. Transforming limited resources into platforms of possibilities begins with two words: "This could…"

"This could…" is a catalyst to reduce waste, increase resiliency, and meet increasing needs using existing resources. There's proven ability in the words. Studies have shown that introducing an object with "This could…" instead of "This is" makes people ten times more likely to find new uses for that object.

"This could…" maximizes our resources by replacing limited assets with an abundance of creativity. The words create new opportunities in a time of budgetary reductions, and new use for existing objects and assets as an alternative to waste and disposal.

It is a tool that will help us realize that increasing our resources doesn't have to mean increasing our consumption of them.

When we were children, we possessed wonderous amounts of imaginative abilities to reimagine anything in the world for new or different use.

Yet as L. A. Vint writes, "As we get older, instead of collecting 'ideas', we begin a process of information elimination. We continue to narrow down our relevance, concerns, curiosity, concentration, and awareness."[6]

Imagine if we were able to reverse this closing down of imagination and began a process of information expansion instead of elimination—expanding our curiosity and awareness of the possibilities that exist in the resources we already have. This book will lead you through the process to give you these abilities.

No particular skill is required to employ "This could..." in any situation, profession, or location. It doesn't matter who you are or what the resource is—the only thing needed is the ability to imagine what something *could be* instead of what it *is*. Where that leads isn't as important as the motion forward. It will lead somewhere.

Not considering what could be done with what we already have leaves us right where we are.

This is not an option.

NEW REWARDS

There's plenty of guilt to go around for the situation we're in—but if you're looking for someone to blame, you'll have to go way back.

When we were hunter-gatherers, there wasn't a lot of contemplation of the impact consumption would have on the future or the environment.

If a wandering group came upon an area bountiful with plants or animals, it was all-hands-on-deck to gather and consume everything possible. Habits that lead to survival tend to stay with us. These certainly did and became deeply embedded in our brain's reward system.

"Unlike what its name may connote, your brain's reward system is not designed to make you feel good," writes Ann-Christine Duhaime in the article *Our Brains Love New Stuff, and It's Killing the Planet.*[7] "The reward system was shaped by what promoted survival during the vast eons of human evolutionary history."

"As a general rule, your brain tweaks you to want more, more, more," notes Duhaime, "because that helped you survive in the distant past."

Those survival-based lessons are the reason why, when faced with a table full of pastries at a social function, resistance seems futile. Our evolutionary instincts tell us to eat the food in front of us because it might be a long time before we find food again.

These same instincts drive us to consume more than just food. If a product is in front of you, online or in person, your survival-prone brain is telling you "What are you waiting for? There it is! Get it…NOW!"

Fortunately, we've picked up plenty of other habits throughout our evolution we can use to change our behavior.

Think of a time when you met a need by employing what you had available at that time: using a steam-filled hotel bathroom to remove the wrinkles from a shirt, using the hinge of a deck chair to open a bottle, or anything you've done to improvise a solution in a moment of need. In these moments, a twinge of satisfaction usually appears.

That small sensation is a big thing. It is your brain's reward system being pleased by a moment of clever problem solving—something our brains find gratifying.

When your reward system gets satisfaction, it receives a dose of dopamine, which our brains *love*. Satisfying your reward system with a moment of ingenuity (and dopamine) helps rewire it away from consumption and towards finding solutions for problems.

"If people who embrace environmental goals treat our evolutionary desires as a puzzle to solve," adds Duhaime, "perhaps we'll get better at working with them to promote sustainability."

Our evolutionary desires need a lot of attention. They are powerful motivators that convince us we need things we don't actually need.

Let's examine a typical motivator for buying something—say, a more powerful computer with x more RAM, or a new phone model with an upgraded processor. The number of people who actually need such speed increases is small, but the number who will buy the more powerful models is large.

The same can be said of automobiles. The 2020 BMW 118i model can go from 0-60 mph in 8 seconds and reach a top speed of 132 mph[8] yet the vast majority of buyers will never experience either of these features while going from points A to B in heavy traffic.

We convince ourselves that we are buying new and more powerful things out of need when in fact, we are buying the perceived *potential* of power instead of the power we actually need.

If the power of potential is one of the key drivers of consumerism, let us work to replace perceived potential with the discovery of actual potential contained in the things we already own and use.

The process isn't a quick flip of a switch, but an iterative process to find satisfaction from your own skills and ingenuity instead of deriving it from a purchase.

When you create a new or improved use for something or contemplate a new opportunity, you are forming new mental connections between resourceful skills and satisfaction.

When this happens, your brain's reward system is pleased, a dose of dopamine is released, and pathways are strengthened that connect resourcefulness with reward—which builds even more ability to perform novel tasks and get satisfaction from them.

Whether making the most of limited budgets or using existing resources in new ways, we already possess the problem-solving skills needed to do more with the assets we have. They got us this far, and we need to rediscover and increase them to help us on the next leg of our journey on this planet.

We can begin by re-establishing a relationship with the material world that surround us.

MATERIAL INTELLIGENCE

"When we made things," Glenn Adamson writes in his book *Fewer, Better Things*, "we accumulated a certain kind of knowledge ... with the severance from this ability we're in danger of losing touch with a knowledge base that allows us to convert raw materials into useful objects, and hand-eye-head-heart-body co-ordination that furnishes us with a meaningful understanding of the materiality of our world."[9]

The knowledge base we're losing touch with is not limited to the materiality of our world. Knowledge of cause and impact is also slipping away.

Food appears in the supermarket; a new product appears on our screen. We consume, buy, discard; a truck comes once a week and our waste disappears.

The collective intelligence of how things work and the impact of our relationship with objects must be resuscitated if we want to have a more resourceful relationship with the world. New gateways of understanding are needed to bring people back into contact with the materiality of things.

A great deal of fault rests in the ease and efficiency we've grown accustomed to as the mechanics of our product-oriented lives have developed.

As Matt Walsh writes for Huffington Post, "Our entire civilization now rests on the assumption that, no matter what else happens, we will all continue to buy lots and lots of things. Buy, buy, buy, buy, buy. And then buy a little more. Don't create, or produce, or discover—just buy."[10]

Adamson echoes this sentiment albeit in a more measured way. "As a culture we are in danger of falling out of touch, not only with objects, but with the intelligence they embody … I am speaking here of material intelligence: a deep understanding of the material world around us, an ability to read that material environment, and the know-how required to give it new form."

Later in this book you will be shown how to deepen your awareness of opportunities that exist to utilize the possibilities and intelligence embedded in objects. The process will help rebuild your material intelligence and the realization that every engagement with a material thing—the purchase, use, repair/reuse, or disposal—is an act that contributes to our current and future life on this planet.

As Adamson concludes, "Our relationship to materials determines much about the way we live on earth. Many people think of themselves as being committed to sustainability, but they focus on a relatively limited set of issues: what type of fish they order at a restaurant, how many airplane trips they take, whether they turn the lights off when they aren't in a room."

"As important as some of those issues are, they pale compared to the impact of the objects we shape and live with. One of the most significant aspects of material intelligence is that it can help us to make better choices about how we live on the planet."[11]

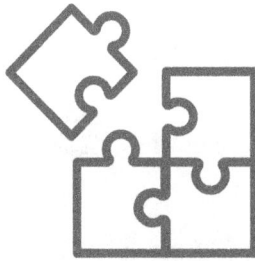

FINDING SOLUTIONS

Understanding that objects, materials, and all existing assets possess intelligence and additional ability is the entry point for a transformative truth:

Everything has the ability to do more than its original function.
For decades I have helped people discover extra abilities contained in assets that make up their businesses, lives, and cities—to find new contexts of use for their content. The benefits of extending the function of something is clear in terms of sustainability. Any object or material repurposed for a new use is one less thing discarded in the earth or ocean.

There is another benefit that is even more valuable—the ability to meet urgent needs using existing assets in new ways.

For all its horrors, the Coronavirus pandemic revealed that a deep well of resourcefulness exists in all of us. When shortcomings were revealed across the social and medical spectrum, many were able to find solutions to urgent needs by using what they already had in new ways.

One example is how one specific resource was reimagined during the pandemic—the parking garage.

Most look at the functional structures and think:

"This is where you park cars."

It's an unfortunate, limited perspective—and one that made little sense when hospitals were running out of room during the pandemic.

In immediate need of additional room for patients and clinical spaces, many hospitals discovered that their parking garages were uniquely suited for additional use.

The structures' bare-bones interiors allowed a rapid transformation of the facilities for medical treatment areas. Their dedicated external entrances and exits and separate ventilation systems proved particularly apt for use during the spread of an airborne virus.

In Reno, Nevada, the Renown Regional Medical Center was searching for a way to quickly increase its ability to handle patients during the pandemic.

As the Reno Gazette Journal reported, "In just 10 days, Renown Regional Medical Center has increased its ability to cope with the spread of COVID-19 by about 173 percent. They've done this by retrofitting the regional trauma center's

Mill Street parking structure into a three-story temporary facility designed to hold 1,400 coronavirus patients at peak capacity."

NBC Washington reported that Mary Washington Hospital was able to repurpose a parking garage into a fully functional medical treatment facility in just over a week:

"They have the space set up to function nearly the same as their normal ER. There is a nurse triage station, laptops for accessing electronic medical records, an HVAC system and a room for X-rays."

So great was the desire for many hospitals to expand medical facilities into parking garages that Walker Consultants issued a guidance article for interested hospitals: *Can Your Parking Garage Provide Hospital Surge Space During the COVID-19 Pandemic?*

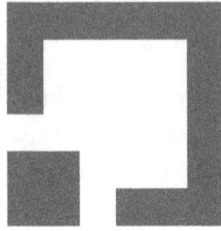

THIS IS vs. THIS COULD

Parking garages are able to meet the urgent needs of medical institutions because they contain extra abilities beyond their prescribed use.

No particular magic lies behind such transformations— utilizing an asset's extra abilities simply requires seeing it with a mindset of "This could…" instead of "This is."

Increasing our awareness of the potential contained in existing objects, structures, or systems is going to be an essential part of a resilient and sustainable future, both ecologically and economically.

Abilities for new use are embedded within almost every physical asset. These resources remain dormant when we limit our perspective to "This is X, and its purpose is to do Y."

If the mental equation is widened to consider, "This is X and its purpose is to do Y, but *this could also do something else,*" an array of new resources and solutions would emerge from what is already there.

When a parking garage is seen with a fixed mindset of "This is," it is simply a place to put cars. But when it is considered with a perspective of "This could..." it is freed from its trappings of prescribed form and function and becomes a resource to meet a need.

Several cities have transformed parking garages into housing, such as The Broadway Autopark in Wichita, Kansas, which transformed a parking structure into 44 living units. Other cities are also beginning to realize the extra capabilities of parking garages. as Axios reports:[12]

- In Chicago, a parking garage under Millennium Park is being converted into an e-commerce delivery logistics center.

- Underground parking garages in LA and other cities are turning into shared commercial kitchens for on-demand, delivery-only food services.

- The roofs of parking garages are being used as urban greenhouses and farms in Denver and Seattle.

- In Paris, an abandoned garage was converted into a growing space for mushrooms and roots that don't need sunlight.

"This could..." is the first step in the process of unlocking additional abilities from any resource.

The words contain a unique energy. Imagine having a conversation with someone about an important issue or business decision. In the middle of the conversation, they pause and say, "This could..." then their phone rings and they take the call while walking out of the room.

The anticipation of what was going to follow those words would be palpable.

"This Could…" activates the mind and builds momentum for new ideas, new options, new directions. It creates an expectation that must be delivered upon.

"This is" sits at the other end of the linguistic spectrum—it is an absolute statement of certainty and fixed identity. No energy builds. No point of departure is expected. Whatever follows is… well, it just is.

Looking at the world with a fixed "This is" mentality leads to, as Albert Einstein said, attempting "solve our problems with the same thinking we used when we created them."

Limited thinking created a path to limited resources and leaves us little to work with going forward.

Seeing everything only in its current state creates a linear, dead-end equation for the future of what we have:

"This Is" x Available Resources = Available Resources

Replacing the limitations of "This is" with the opportunities "This could…" unleashes, changes the equation:

"This Could…" x Available Resources = Additional Resources

Swapping *Is* for *Could* is just a one-word exchange that unlocks potential. It transforms the capability of existing assets from dormant objects to dynamic containers of possibility.

● ● ●

WHAT HAS "THIS COULD..." DONE FOR US?

The world is filled with innovations born from someone looking at an object, material, or system, and thinking, "This could...," then following the path opened by those words.

The iPhone

In 1971, a friend called John Draper to share a discovery. A toy whistle packaged inside Captain Crunch cereal emitted a perfect 2600 hertz tone when blown—the same frequency that telephone operators use to authenticate themselves when connecting to the central exchange.

The friend explained that if someone dialed the number of a phone exchange and blew the whistle into the phone when the call connected, the exchange would think it was an operator calling and allow full access to the phone network. Draper understood the potential of the toy whistle.

"This could unlock America's phone system."

A few months later Draper built "blue boxes" that reproduced the whistle's frequency. A university student named Steve Wozniak read an article about Draper and his blue boxes and invited Draper to his dorm room to learn about them firsthand.

When Draper arrived, he found that Wozniak had invited a friend to join them named Steve Jobs.

After a demo of the blue box's abilities and a tutorial on how to make them, Wozniak and Jobs decided to go into business together making blue boxes—with Wozniak making them and Jobs selling them. It was the beginning of a working relationship and an early source of funding that led to them founding Apple.

There's delightful irony in the fact that today's icon of telecommunications, the iPhone, can be traced back to someone blowing a toy whistle into a rotary phone and thinking "This could…"

Nike

In 1970 runners were having a hard time adjusting to the University of Oregon's new urethane track. Metal spikes would rip it up, and the day's ordinary running shoes provided insufficient traction.

Track coach Bill Bowerman was searching for alternatives that would work equally well on the track and other surfaces. He had already formed a company with former member of his track team Phil Knight to distribute running shoes, but with operating costs soaring and a fraying relationship with their supplier, they agreed that the time had come to make their own shoe.

One Sunday morning in 1971 Bowerman and his wife Barbara were having breakfast together in their kitchen. Bowerman was still fixated on creating a better running shoe and Barbara was making waffles. As she recalled:

"As one of the waffles came out, he said, 'You know, by turning it upside down—where the waffle part would come in contact with the track—I think that might work.' So, he got up from the table and went tearing into his lab and got two cans of whatever it is you pour together to make the urethane and poured them into the waffle iron[13]." In that moment, Bowerman realized:

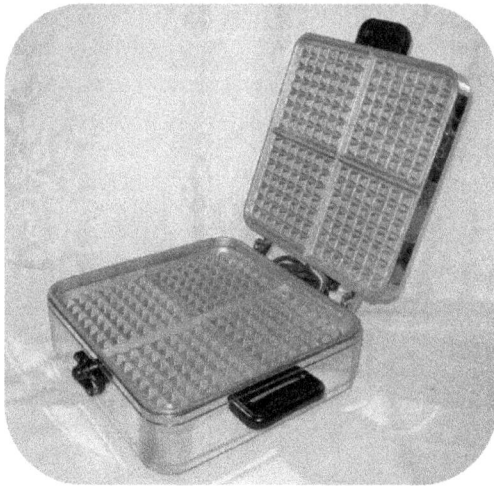

"This could make a better running shoe."

The result—after several ruined waffle irons—was a shoe tread that didn't tear up the track and gripped every type of running surface.

Nike's "Waffle Trainer" debuted in 1974 and gave the company (wait for it) the traction to become one of the world's most successful sports brands.

Play-Doh

Prior to WWII many households were heated with coal, which left a dark sticky residue on walls. Efforts to clean it with available products would only make things worse, smearing painted walls or ruining paper wallpaper.

Kroger's grocery stores in Cincinnati, Ohio, commissioned a company to find a solution. Kutol was the answer—a pliable, putty-like material that would draw the coal residue off walls without damage. It reigned supreme as the wall cleaner of the time.

Then coal stoves were replaced with residue-free gas stoves and homes began decorating with vinyl wallpaper that could be cleaned with regular products. As homes changed, so did Kutol's fortunes.

One day nursery schoolteacher Kay Zufall read a newspaper article about making art with Kutol and thought:

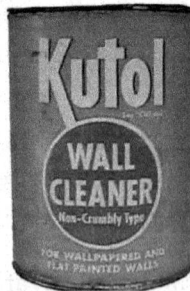

"This could be a great toy."

She bought a can, added some food coloring, and gave it to her students to play with.

The children loved it. They sculpted it, created creatures with it, rolled it out, and used cookie cutters to create shapes.

Zufall's new use for Kutol could have faded into history if not for a fortuitous connection: she was the sister-in-law of Joe McVicker, nephew of Kutol's founder.

Zufall shared her new use for Kutol with McVicker and persuaded him and company founder Noah McVicker to reconsider it as a child's toy. The McVickers recognized its potential and retooled the company to produce "Rainbow Modeling Compound."

Zufall's new use for the wall cleaner transformed the company's fortunes—but she had one last contribution to make to toy history when she told them:

"You should call it 'Play-Doh'."

For every one of these documented moments, countless others have occurred in sheds, workshops, barns, and households that improved something, for someone, in some way.

All were born from the same two words: "This could…"

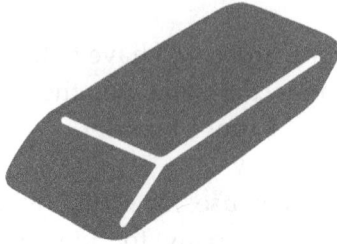

THIS COULD BE A RUBBER BAND

There is quantifiable evidence of the difference "This could…" makes.

In 1987, Harvard psychologists Ellen J. Langer and Alison I. Piper performed a series of experiments to explore the difference a "single linguistic variation" could have on people's perception of objects. They were curious if the ability to think creatively would increase if participants were introduced to objects in a conditional way ("This could be X") instead of with an absolute term ("This is X").

In one experiment, participants were divided into two groups. Participants in the first group were given a rubber band and told:

"**This is** a rubber band."

Members of the second group were also given a rubber band. In this group, however, each person was told:

"**This could** be a rubber band."

Both groups were then told they had to perform a task that required an eraser, but no erasers were available. In the group that was introduced to the rubber band with an absolute statement ("This is"):

3 percent realized it could be used as an eraser.

In the group that were introduced to the rubber band with a conditional statement ("This could"):

40 percent realized it could be used as an eraser.

As Langer and Piper summarized, by using the conditional "This could" when introducing participants to the rubber band instead of the absolute "This is", "A different need was then generated for which the object in question was not explicitly suited but could fulfill."

"Introducing people to a new part of their world in this conditional manner resulted in more mindful use of that information," wrote Langer and Piper. Participants in the "This could" group, "were able to use the unfamiliar object creatively when the need arose."

They noted that participants who were introduced to the rubber band with the absolute term "This is" appeared to make "premature cognitive commitments" to the use of the rubber band.

"Because of the absolute way in which it was initially presented," they wrote, participants had a difficult time breaking from its singular identity and use. When they needed an eraser, the absolute term made them assume that the rubber band was "not able to meet this need."

The study shows the impact language can have on our perception of an object's identity and use. "This is" imposed a rigid framework of use upon the students. "This could" released the students' perceptions from the object's fixed identity and use and freed them to think of other uses for the rubber band.

CONDITIONAL THINKING

The ability to view things conditionally gives us the freedom to change our perspective of the material world—and frees our objects from their prescribed use.

"This could…" creates an awareness of different contexts and possibilities by creating a conditional understanding of things.

As Langer writes, "A conditional understanding of the world seems to prevent mindlessness."

Mindlessness is the biggest stumbling block in the pursuit of a more resourceful relationship with existing objects, materials, and resources. As Langer and Piper write in their later study *The Prevention of Mindlessness*, "Mindlessness is marked by a rigid use of information during which the individual is not aware of its potentially novel aspects … One deals with information as though it has a single meaning and is available for use in only that way."

Most of us cruise through the day in a mindless state, paying attention only to work or tasks that demand focus. We fail to register opportunities that exist in our periphery as we go about our daily routine.

We lose touch with our surroundings and imagination when we are merely functional during the day and fail to recognize the value in our periphery.

To recognize and utilize the potential that exists in everyday experiences, we must avoid mindlessness and strive to have a more mindful awareness of the world around us.

"When we are mindful," writes Langer and Piper, "we are actively drawing novel distinctions, rather than relying on distinctions drawn in the past. This makes us sensitive to context and perspective...our behavior may be guided rather than governed by rules and routines, but we are sensitive to the ways the situation changes."[14]

Our minds constantly take us back and forth in time. Mindlessness occupies our brain with information from the past—fixed use, fixed identities, and rote solutions, keeping us in a loop that obscures opportunities.

Mindfulness keeps us in the present. Rules and routines from the past still exist, but being mindful of the present moment lets us re-interpret and reframe past information according to the needs we have now. Being fully aware of the context and perspective of the here and now allows us to think conditionally and explore opportunity.

An example of the potential of mindfulness and conditional thinking at work is what takes place in the minds of London's Black Cab drivers.

To get their license, drivers must pass a test known as "The Knowledge." The Knowledge requires three to four years of study during which the drivers must memorize 25,000 streets, thousands of tourist attractions, and frequently requested destinations.

Just committing the streets to memory isn't enough. Drivers are obligated to take passengers from points A to B using the quickest route possible.

This level of mastery reveals itself when you take a Black Cab trough London. The destination you requested when entering the cab has a fixed route according to a map and the driver knows it well.

But as the cab's wheels roll, so do the wheels in the driver's mind—constantly re-mapping the route in real time, responding to the variables of time of day, traffic congestion, road closures, and so on.

The driver is plying his trade in a conditional manner, constantly re-working options based on current contexts of need (getting to the passenger's destination) and opportunity (navigating the fastest possible route).

The benefit gained from years of memorization and conditional behavior was revealed during a study of London's cab drivers. Reporting on the research of Neuroscientist Eleanor Maguire, Scientific American magazine reports[15]:

"Maguire discovered that London taxi drivers had more gray matter in their posterior hippocampi than people who were similar in age, education and intelligence, but who did not drive taxis."

"It seemed that the longer someone had been driving a taxi, the larger his hippocampus, as though the brain expanded to accommodate the cognitive demands of navigating London's streets."

As Neurobiologist Howard Eichenbaum writes regarding the taxi drivers, "It turns out it was the training process that caused the growth in the brain. It shows you can produce profound changes in the brain with training. That's a big deal."

You don't need to spend years navigating London's streets to increase your brain's capacity. The steps later in this book will give you a chance to increase your own conditional thinking abilities, change the way you perceive opportunity, and yes, grow your brain in the process.

Everyone has found themselves in a situation where a need arises at the most inconvenient time. In these moments, you instinctively begin viewing the objects around you in a conditional context. What *could* be used to help me right now? A spark of ingenuity often appears that amplifies the utility of what you have then and there.

When you accessed those innermost skills the solution to your need began by contemplating something you had at hand and thinking "This could…"

Such moments of need and resolution have become less frequent as 24/7 services and on-demand assistance increase and our need for self-reliance decreases.

In the past, utilizing available resources to meet a need was commonplace. Resourcefulness was a skill you, your family, and your livelihood depended upon. It's just what you did.

THE FARMER'S PHONE SYSTEM

When telephones first appeared in the early 1900s companies were only interested in building networks for cities. Rural settlements were too sparsely populated and remote to justify investment in the wire, poles, equipment, and manpower needed to connect them.

But because of their remote locations and dispersed populations farmers had real needs for a telephone. Phones would allow them to get help during emergencies, share weather reports with other farmers, and simply talk and connect with one another to battle rural isolation.

So, farmers took matters into their own hands.

The early telephone system was little more than basic devices for speaking and listening, and junction boxes connected by a network of wires. Some explored ways in which they could replicate this system on their own.

They bought the phone units and junction boxes. For the network required to connect them they realized one was already in place: barbed wire fences.

Lost to history is the name of the person who looked at the miles of fence wire stretching across the prairie and thought:

"This could be a phone network."

Some farmers would run special phone wires along the top of existing fences. Others would use the existing barbed wire for the phone network. Junction boxes were installed in kitchens or the local post office. As Lynne Hayes describes in an article for *Growing America*:[16]

"Typically, a smooth wire was strung from a telephone in a house or barn to a barbed wire fence. From there, it hooked into the top strand of barbed wire (most fences had at least three strands) and the telephone signal would follow the length of the wire to a second telephone that was connected to the barbed wire down the line."

"With thousands of miles of barbed wire fencing spanning the country in the early 1900s, all the makings of this crude system were already in place."

The "Farmer's Phone System" is an early manifestation of "This could…" thinking—looking at an existing asset (the barbed wire fence system) and realizing it could meet a need (for a phone network).

At its peak, over three million people across the Midwest were connected by fence wire phones—more than were connected by the official Bell system.[17]

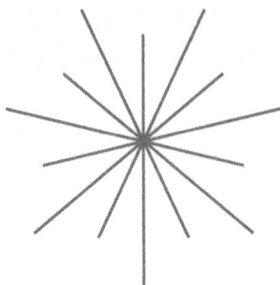

THE MARVELOUS IMPLICIT IN THE EVERYDAY

The farmers who turned fences into a phone network were already primed to find new uses for existing assets—reuse and resourcefulness were common skills at the time.

We no longer rely on such depths of resourcefulness to get by, but it is still within us, deposited there by previous generations just as evolutionary traits like fight or flight remain deep within, ready to be activated when needed.

For proof that such ingenuity is within our DNA, we don't need to look any further than our children. When they interact with the world, objects adults would consider ordinary become capable of new realities:

"This could… be a horse, a baseball bat, a sword…"

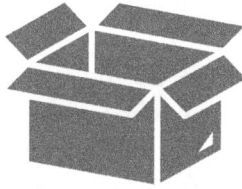

"This could... be a time machine, a spaceship, a fort..."

These alternate realities are often dismissed as "products of a child's imagination," without recognizing the significance of the conditional thinking taking place.

As we grow into adulthood our world becomes defined by fixed perspectives. We are taught that objects and materials have specific identities and uses. This process is a necessary part of learning about the world, but it creates collateral damage.

At some point in our development a playful use of an object is met with a correction: "That's *not* what that is for." As more of these moments occur over time, the imagination closes down and never fully recovers.

In the late 1960s NASA wanted to measure the creativity of their rocket scientists. They commissioned Dr. George Land and Beth Jarman to develop a creativity test to measure "divergent thinking"—the ability to look at a situation, problem, or object and come up with different solutions or alternate ways to meet a need. For example, "Name as many uses as you can for this jar of paper clips."

Some would come up with multiple additional uses for the jar, some would find other uses for the paper clips, and so on.

The premise was that the more possibilities an individual came up with, the more creative they were.

In 1968 the same study was conducted on 1,600 preschool children aged three to five who were enrolled in a Head Start program. In following years, the students were given the same test at age 10, and again when they were 15.

The results reveal what happens to levels of creativity with age. The percentage of participants who scored as "highly creative" at each age level were as follows:

> *Test results amongst 5-year-olds: 98%*
> *Test results amongst 10-year-olds: 30%*
> *Test results amongst 15-year-olds: 12%*
> *Same test given to 280,000 adults (average age being 31): 2%*

"What we have concluded," wrote Land, "is that non-creative behavior is learned."[18] As we grow, creativity is not learned as much as it is unlearned. The myth that some people are born creative is more accurately stated that some are able to *remain* creative as they grow.

We cannot pretend to throw a switch and become five years old again in our mind, but we can work to free our mind from the trappings of certainty and fixed identity. We can re-engage with something we once had in abundance: an open, curious mind.

"Curiosity is what makes us try something until we can do it, or think about something until we understand it," writes Erika Andersen in the article *Learning to Learn*.[19]

"Great learners retain this childhood drive or regain it through another application of self-talk. Instead of focusing on and reinforcing initial disinterest in a new subject, they learn to ask themselves 'curious questions' about it and follow those questions up with actions."

"This could…" is a form of curious questioning that, when followed by actions, can have a profound impact on the world. Yet it is not nurtured throughout our development.

Most of us are the product of a 200-year-old education system that taught us to be good followers of rules and recipients of fixed learnings. Along the way, we lost touch with the abilities of our imagination—and as Albert Einstein put it, "Imagination is more important than knowledge."

In his collection of essays *Shame and Wonder*, David Searcy recalls the wonder he felt as a young man when he saw "Hot Rods" on display. The magic for Searcy was:

"They were not like concept cars, those empty visions of the future that manufacturers like to roll out on occasion. These were ordinary cars transformed. Revealed, in a way, as what they ought to be … The marvelous implicit in the everyday."

Approaching the world with a mindset of "This could…" allows Searcy's wonderful phrase, "The marvelous implicit in the everyday" to come to life.

FRISBIE!

In the early 1900s, the Frisbie Pie Company in Bridgeport, Connecticut, was doing brisk business selling pies from its trucks.

Managers looked at their mobile pie operation and saw a good business. The pie salesmen saw something different.

Returning to a neighborhood where they had sold pies days earlier, they saw kids flinging empty pie pans to each other.

To warn people that a metal disc was about to be airborne, the kids would yell "Frisbie!" as they threw.

The original Frisbee, circa 1920.

Several years later Fredrick Morrison saw kids throwing the pie plates back and forth and was inspired to design a more aerodynamic—and impact friendly—disc from plastic. He patented his "Pluto Platter" flying saucer toy and sold it to toy company Wham-O.

The company paid tribute to the discs origins by renaming it "Frisbee," and the rest is beach and backyard history.

A pie plate became the Frisbee we know today because of the abilities it contained beyond its prescribed identity and use, and because of a group of kids who understood this.

The Frisbie pie plate had a set identity: it was a pie plate. Its function was also set: it held pies.

The kids that picked up an empty Frisbie pie plate knew what it was and what it was *supposed to be for*, but their agile minds saw past those definitions and thought, "This could be used for *something else.*"

The extra abilities of a pie plate enabled the Frisbee to be created.

There are additional abilities contained in many objects whose use and identity we take for granted. Realizing everything is in a fluid state between current and future use allows an object's extra abilities to emerge.

As Jake Silverstein writes in *The New York Times Magazine*, "No design is ever permanent but merely a way station between what a thing used to be and what it might yet become."

Opportunity suffocates in minds closed off by old notions and certainties. The Frisbee story holds an important lesson:

Put a pie plate the hands of those with an agile mind and it will lead to a Frisbee.

Put a pie plate in the hands of those with locked minds and it will lead to another pie.

RESOURCE-AWARE SOLUTIONS

"Our lives once comprised an almost unbroken chain of movements and actions as we interacted physically with the material requirements of our existence," writes Alexander Langlands in his book *Craeft*. "Today we stare at screens and we press buttons."

The shift to a digital relationship with reality has skewed our relationship with physical resources. A CAD operator can easily add another 10 floors to a building or expand its footprint without having to directly engage with the physical resources assigned by those actions.

The same for the product designer, engineer, or any profession whose digital design is the first link in the resource consumption chain. Each will have an understanding and awareness of their impact, but are making decisions without resources at hand or within sight.

"When man first began to build," writes Christopher Williams in the book *Craftsmen of Necessity*, "from the surroundings came his materials: the plants and animals, the rock and dirt. He converted the materials into his tools. He learned the vernacular of his materials, the strength of wood, the shapes of clay, the cleavage of stone. He learned the pressures and demands of the biosphere, and he bent to them."

We no longer need to source tools and materials from the raw materials of nature, but the need to bend to the pressures and demands of the biosphere has never been more vital.

"Innovation" has become a catch-all solution to pull any problem out of the abyss. Throw innovation at a problem and... problem solved. But innovation takes time; it takes resources—two things that aren't always in ample supply when problems arise, particularly urgent ones, as was evident during the early stages of the Coronavirus pandemic.

"We are told that innovation is the most important force in our economy, the one thing we must get right or be left behind," writes David Sax in *End the Innovation Obsession*[20].

"But that fear of missing out has led us to foolishly embrace the false trappings of innovation over truly innovative ideas that may be simpler and ultimately more effective... Often that actually means adopting ideas and tools that already exist but make sense in a new context."

We need to pull back from assuming the magic of innovation will provide answers, and instead explore ways to craft solutions from the resources we already have.

We have plenty of problems and needs, but we don't have plenty of material, financial, spatial, and natural resources to meet those needs.

We do, however, have plenty of resources that lie dormant, discarded, and under-utilized.

"This could..." represents resource-aware innovation, where existing resources become the raw material for new use, understanding, and problem solving.

In the 1700s shipping created enormous wealth and opened nations to the world. For all the benefits it provided, seafaring crews were given few resources beyond their own resourcefulness if their ship was damaged and ran aground.

In 1783 Charles-Joseph Panckoucke published an illustration in his Marine Encyclopedia to make it easier to find parts to build and repair a ship when the need arose.

Marine

Using the illustration, sailors and shipwrights could go into the woods and, seeing a tree with a long, straight trunk think, "This could be the ship's mast." Coming upon a tree with solid, sturdy forks at the base of branches would spur the thought, "This could be the buttress for the bow."

The illustration is an early visual guide for resource-aware thinking to meet a need: how to identify trees that could provide parts for a ship. It is also an early example showing people how to look at existing physical assets with "This could..." in mind.

When the COVID-19 pandemic struck, it was awareness of extra abilities contained in existing resources that created new channels of supplies and assistance to help people through a time of great uncertainty and vulnerability.

From Spirits to Sanitizer

Many restaurants and bars were forced to close as states fought to control the spread of the Coronavirus.

The ones who were able operate could only do so with a small percentage of usual patron occupancy. Some saw the time as a struggle to remain in business—others saw it as an opportunity to pivot their resources and meet the growing needs of the time.

Colorado's Marble Distilling company realized they had all the equipment and processes required to pivot from producing alcohol to manufacturing hand sanitizer. With a supply of raw materials already in place, "We only needed one additive to be able to make a hand sanitizer," said co-founder Carey Shanks.[21] "The transition was very quick."

New York Distilling Company in Brooklyn created a recipe for hand sanitizer using its Perry's Tot Navy Strength Gin that met CDC recommendations. "We thought, at least this is a reasonable way to put ourselves to some use," Allen Katz, co-founder and owner of New York Distilling Company, told *Men's Health Magazine*.

"We have access to off-the-still gin made in our Brooklyn distillery that we can turn into a homemade sanitizer that meets CDC recommendations. We can use our resources to help support friends in the hospitality and trade who are in need right now."

In Vermont, Caledonia Spirits converted their production facilities to make hand sanitizer for local nonprofit organizations such as the Vermont Foodbank, which then gave the sanitizer to employees and stocked it in their food pantry for the public.

"For our recipe, we're following the guidelines set forth by the World Health Organization, so our hand sanitizer is just as effective as what you can buy in the store," said Caledonia Spirits VP of Marketing Harrison Kahn in a release.

A range of companies recognized the extra abilities of their manufacturing operations and available resources and put them to use to meet needs caused by the pandemic:

- Organic bedding company Avocado shifted the cut and sew department in their Los Angeles factory to make reusable organic face masks.

- Dyson developed a ventilator designed specifically for COVID-19 patients. With its seasoned team of engineers and designers, the company was able to design the ventilator in just 10 days.

- Loll Designs, a maker of outdoor furniture, designed a recyclable hospital bed. Using materials already in stock, they were able to make on-demand beds for hospitals suddenly overwhelmed by the crisis.

School Bus Wi-Fi

The school year was in full swing when the pandemic hit the US and classes had to quickly move online. This presented its own set of challenges, from the effectiveness of online instruction to student attention span while staring at a screen.

For some students, there was a more fundamental challenge to online learning—a lack of high-speed internet. Schools didn't have the financial resources to provide necessary internet access to every low-income student, but they did have another resource that could be used to meet the need: a fleet of school busses, many of which were already Wi-Fi-enabled.

As School Transportation News reported:

"With the recent surge in school closures due to COVID-19, these buses are no longer transporting students. But the Internet access they provide is not going to waste. Districts have started re-purposing their Wi-Fi-equipped buses to create community Internet hotspots for students and their families."

"The Austin [Texas] Independent School District strategically deployed over 100 of their Wi-Fi-equipped buses into neighborhoods and apartment complexes where the district identified the highest need for Internet access. The buses are parked throughout the community from 8:00 a.m. to 2:00 p.m., Monday through Friday."

School districts joined together and assigned busses across regions to apportion Wi-Fi access as needed. Some buses would be stationed in parking lots so parents could drive up within range to allow their children to go online for specific classes or online course needs.

Coffee Filter Masks

When the pandemic first spread through Europe in early 2020, protective medical supplies and masks quickly ran short.

German authorities made a public appeal for more masks, and help came from an unlikely source: Melitta, the 122-year-old German maker of coffee filters.

The company realized that by reimagining the potential of their existing materials and production capabilities they could produce up to a million masks a day.

As The New York Times reports, "The essential ingredient in many medical-grade masks—what separates them from simple homemade versions—is a filter made of nonwoven super thin fibers, formed in a process known as melt-blown extrusion. Since the pandemic, demand for so-called melt-blown fiber has skyrocketed. For Melitta, melt-blown fiber is readily available: It makes its own, mainly for use in vacuum cleaner bags."

The company's supply of the necessary microfiber normally used in vacuum cleaner bags was the first of two assets it re-assigned for mask production. The second was the process for making and shaping coffee filters, as their shape proved fortuitous for their new use.

As Katharina Roehrig, a managing director at Melitta, told The New York Times, "The ergonomics of the thing, the fact that the filter fits exactly over mouth, nose and chin is so unbelievable that you might call it a gift from heaven."

By swapping their machines' source material from coffee filter fiber to the fiber used in vacuum cleaners, Melitta was able to produce masks with a filter efficiency above 98 percent, comparable to medical masks.

In the first month Melitta was able to produce 10 million protective masks using its existing assets in new ways.

INCREASING RESOURCES

Throughout history we've been very good at increasing our use of resources to meet our increasing needs. So good, in fact, it has become instinctive.

The problem is that our instinct to meet new needs by using more resources is no longer a realistic solution. It's a difficult situation to navigate.

The global population is growing, and growing populations have growing needs. In our personal lives, we grow from infants to children to adults, and along the way, we need more.

There's a need for more resources without any assurances that there always will be more available. What is needed is the ability to increase resources without increasing consumption of them. It seems a paradoxical challenge, but one that is achievable.

The journey begins categorizing resources into two types: external and internal.

External Resources

External resources are the things we use or rely on to do our jobs, meet a challenge, or respond to a need: objects, fuel, materials, technology, tools, mechanical assistance, and so on.

There are many types of external resources, but all share one trait: regardless of their origin or form, they are limited.

Natural resources become depleted, physical materials are consumed, mechanical apparatus require energy and fuel and wear out over time. In addition, acquiring external resources almost always involves an expenditure of sorts, either financial or material.

There is a limit to the supply and longevity of external resources and constraints in terms of access—every *thing* has to reside somewhere. Employing external resources relies on having access to those things.

Most importantly, moments of vulnerability and risk can increase when there is an over-reliance on external resources to provide solutions. In moments of urgent need, external resources can be unstable and unpredictable, for reasons already noted.

Internal Resources

Internal resources are the capabilities we acquire over time: experience, knowledge, technical ability, perception, skills, insight, and so on. They are investments we make in ourselves.

Internal resources are not confined by the same limitations as external resources. There are always more abilities and skills to acquire, more insight and experience to be gained.

Most importantly, the value of these two resources changes with their use. External resources decrease in capability and value as they are used and exhausted—physical resources become depleted with use, mechanical resources exhaust with time.

Internal resources, however, increase over time. As they are used, they grow in ability and value. Internal resources provide freedom and an agility of response—they are always with us and ready for use as needed.

As our internal resources increase, so do the capabilities of our external resources. Honing our ability to see external resources in terms of what they *could be* and *could do* beyond their current state increases their abilities to meet our needs.

By increasing our internal resources, external resources increase their capacity without necessitating an increase in their consumption.

When you close this book, you will have more internal resources, which will allow you to do more with your external resources, and will decrease your reliance on them to meet current and future needs.

Ready to get to work?

SECTION TWO

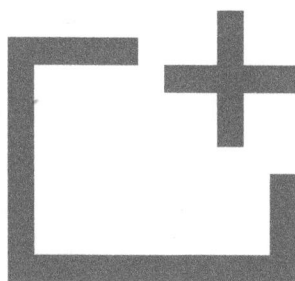

HOW TO DO MORE WITH WHAT YOU HAVE

Now things get real. It's time to learn how to do more with what you already have. Six sections follow that will guide you through a process of letting go of limited perspectives, learning how to see opportunity, and doing more with your existing resources. Here's what the journey looks like:

Step 1: Let Go

Step 2: Learn to See

Step 3: Use New Words

Step 4: Consider Components

Step 5: Create New Contexts

Step 6: Shift Skills

Throughout the sections are examples and worksheets. A pdf of the worksheets is available here:

https://thiscould.com/downloads/Worksheets.pdf

STEP 1: LET GO

There was once a wise Zen master whom people would seek for his counsel and wisdom. Many would come and ask him to teach and enlighten them in the way of Zen. One day a wealthy businessman visited the master.

"I have come today to ask you to teach me about Zen. Open my mind to enlightenment," he commanded. The Zen master nodded and said they should begin by having a cup of tea.

The master began pouring tea into the man's cup. As he poured, the tea rose above the rim and spilled over onto the table. The man shouted "Enough! You are spilling the tea! Can't you see the cup is full?"

The master stopped pouring. He looked at the man and pointed to the cup. "You are like this teacup, so full that nothing more can be added. Come back to me with an empty mind."

It's tough to empty your cup, but doing so brings rewards.

When the pandemic first rattled the economy, financial advisors offered tips for coping with a period of financial uncertainty. Those who were able, most said, should reduce their credit card debt and negotiate interest rates to "lighten the load" going forward.

The same advice applies to the mental loads we carry as we work towards a better future. Concerns and convictions accumulated over time pull us away from the present and into the past.

We have to let go of the past in ways big and small to realize the next chapter of our relationship with things. Greater agility and creativity come to those who are able to lighten their loads.

Neuroscientist Moshe Bar and researcher Shira Baror studied the relationship between mental loads and creativity. In one experiment they asked two groups to memorize a string of numbers—one group had to memorize seven digits, the other just two. Each group was then asked to perform a series of word associations while keeping the numbers in mind.

Bar and Baror found that the participants with the "high mental load" of seven digits delivered the most typical responses (e.g., white/black), while those with less on their mind—having to remember only two digits—gave more varied and creative responses (e.g., white/cloud).

"These experiments," wrote Barr, "suggest that the mind's natural tendency is to explore and to favor novelty, but when occupied it looks for the most familiar and inevitably least interesting solution."[22]

We've all had a great idea while in the shower or out walking. In these moments the mind is usually in a quiet state—simply focused on the feeling of water on your skin or a blowing breeze. Free space provides room for ideas and insight to flow.

If you want to try and reduce the mental noise of churning thoughts, a limitless amount of advice, programs, and apps are out there that promise to lower your mental load, reduce your stress, and increase your creativity. Explore and find what works for you—I recommend meditation, but to each their own.

In the short term, there is something you can do every day to pause churning thoughts and anchor yourself in the present. It's quick, it's easy, and it is always available:

Be where you are.

Most of us cruise on "autopilot" as we go about our days, detached from the world around us. The more familiar the place and routine, the more we mindlessly glide through it.

In the moments when our eyes and hands aren't required to be in action, we reach for our phones—in line at a coffee shop, waiting to cross the street, or sitting or standing on the bus or subway. Give someone a moment of pause and they will most likely spend it staring at a screen.

It is difficult to change such ingrained habits. What we need to be aware of, however, is what spending our time on autopilot and being lost in a screen robs from us: awareness and contemplation.

The world is brimming with untapped potential contained in its existing assets. The more distracted we are from our surrounding environment, the more opportunities we miss.

An engineer waiting for the subway one day wasn't passing the time staring at a phone but observing the dynamics of a subway car approached the platform.

The screech of the breaks as the train came to a stop sparked an idea: the friction occurring during breaking could be harnessed as a power source.

The technique is now used on subway trains in Philadelphia and other cities. As Popular Mechanics reports, "When subway trains in Philadelphia slam on the brakes, they'll also be sending power to the grid."[23]

We rarely give ourselves time to observe our surroundings and contemplate the opportunities it contains. The more time spent staring at screens or operating on autopilot during daily tasks the more detached we become.

Similarly, we've become detached from what happens to our waste and discarded gadgets. We just get rid of the things we don't want and buy more.

We've become detached from where things come from, how they're made, and how we can fix them. We live in this world but often fail to be active, conscious participants in its material contents.

Many modern conveniences separate us from the real world. A recent survey discovered that 66 percent of people under the age of 25 are unable to read paper maps due to reliance on GPS and step-by-step directions offered by their phone.

We can't be paying attention to potential opportunities that exist around us when we're obediently following turn by turn instructions or are lost in a few inches of a phone screen.

If Newton had a smart phone when he was sitting under the apple tree, we might still be wondering why things fall.

Being fully present in the moment is only part of what is needed to engage with opportunities that surround you. The other is to be able to view them with a fresh perspective—to move beyond your previous assumptions and let new realities emerge.

Learn to Unlearn

For new ideas and opportunities to reveal themselves, you have to move beyond learnings from the past.

You have to learn to unlearn.

"Unlearning is not about forgetting," Mark Bonchek writes in the Harvard Business Review. "It's about the ability to choose an alternative mental model or paradigm. When we learn, we add new skills or knowledge to what we already know. When we unlearn, we step outside the mental model in order to choose a different one."

Psychologist Herbert Gerjuoy of the Human Resources Research Organization notes, "When we unlearn, we generate anew rather than reformulate the same old stuff. Creativity and innovation bubble up during the process of unlearning."

"Once we remove our blinders, the world becomes quite different, with new possibilities and innovative approaches to situations that previously seemed stale or difficult."[24]

If the word "unlearning" doesn't work for you, use a different one: discovering, reimagining, reinterpreting, whatever you want. The label doesn't matter—expanding your perception of the world and its untapped possibilities is the important thing. Because what you already know can be a barrier to what you want to learn.

As Dee Hock, founder and former CEO of Visa once said, "The problem is never how to get new, innovative thoughts into your mind, but how to get the old ones out."

Increasing creativity by unlearning has been at the forefront of business thinking for some time.

In 1956, Louis R. Mobley was asked to create a school for IBM's business executives. Writing in Forbes Magazine, August Turak, who cites Mobley as a mentor, reflects on Mobley's discoveries about creativity while running the IBM Executive School:

"Becoming creative is an unlearning rather than a learning process. The goal of the IBM Executive School was not to add more assumptions but to upend existing assumptions … that, 'Wow, I never thought of it that way before!' reaction that is the birth pang of creativity."

Think of a time when you were so certain of a way of process or piece of information you knew there was only one path to follow: yours. The certainty you felt wasn't a product of the current moment, it was a remnant from the past—something previously learned.

Then a new piece of information was presented, and you changed course. The new information was a product of the present and you grew because of it.

Many remain blind to new discoveries because they are stuck in previous certainties and identities. It is difficult to be truly innovative when cut off from the numerous channels of possibility and opportunity that are obscured by previous layers of assumption.

Example: SuKuLTuR

German publishing company Geile Warenautomaten GmbH was looking for new ways to distribute its SuKuLTuR book series *Beautiful Reading*.

One day, someone from the company was waiting for a train on the Berlin subway when an empty space in a vending machine sparked a thought. Instead of just selling sweets:

"This could also sell books."

The company approached the machine's operator and within a few months 11 subway vending machines were distributing five different editions of the *Beautiful Reading* series.

As the company says on its website, "At these vending machines you could now buy not only wine gum, chocolate bars, chewing gum, marble cake and other sweets, but also fine literature. For just one Euro."

"If you are waiting for one of the elevated trains in Berlin, you ought to scout the vending machines," writes Dorothea von Moltke in the Wild River Review.

"Not because German potato chips are better than any others or because the Twix has an aftertaste of cinnamon in the Berlin air, but because displayed between the two snacks, you are liable to find a bright yellow pamphlet: food for thought during the time it takes to travel between most points A and B in this wide, flat city."

After selling more than 100,000 copies of the editions— designed specifically to fit vending machine slots—the company expanded nationwide throughout Germany's rail system with its own line of book vending machines.

This trajectory was only possible because when the person saw the empty space in the machine, they were able to let go of their past understanding of what a vending machine was *supposed to do*—what it was *supposed to sell*—and understood the opportunity that existed in what it *could do*.

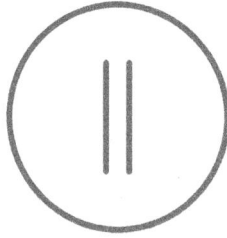

STEP 2: LEARN TO SEE

"We don't see things as they are; we see them as we are."

- Anaïs Nin

To discover new opportunities, we have to build new capabilities—capabilities that are better, stronger, faster... (cue *Six Million Dollar Man* theme song).

This requires learning to see. Not improving the ability of your optic nerves, but training your mind to see your surroundings with full awareness. It takes work.

As Gene Tracy writes in American Scientist[25], "Learning to see is not an innate gift; it is an iterative process, always in flux and constituted by the culture in which we find ourselves and the tools we have to hand."

Don't beat yourself up if you have trouble with this at first. Some of the most highly skilled professionals can be blind to things right in front of them.

This is known as "inattentional blindness," a phenomenon that occurs when observers are so focused on a task and locked into fixed perceptions they become oblivious to extraneous stimuli.

"When engaged in a demanding task, attention can act like a set of blinders, making it possible for stimuli to pass, undetected, right in front of our eyes," said Trafton Drew, Ph.D. "Even experts are vulnerable to this phenomenon."

Drew is lead author of a study from Brigham and Women's Hospital[26] showing that highly trained professionals can fail to see objects others would consider obvious. In this case, the professionals were unable to see a gorilla.

In the experiment, 24 radiologists were asked to examine five different pulmonary X-ray scans for a routine lung node detection task. As Medical Daily reports:[27]

"Each scan contained an average of ten lung nodules. However, in the fifth scan, researchers added something that generally does not appear in X-rays: a gorilla."

"The layered silhouette of a giant ape, 48 times larger than a lung nodule, appeared at the top corner of the scan. While eye-movement tracking measures indicated that most subjects stared right at it, a menacing 83 percent failed to register what they were actually looking at."

"The radiologists missed the gorillas," said Jeremy Wolfe, senior psychologist and director of the Visual Attention Laboratory at Brigham and Women's Hospital, "not because they could not see them, but because the way their brains had framed what they were doing."

"People only see what they are prepared to see."

- Ralph Waldo Emerson

We all have moments when we fail to see everything. Your brain instinctively focuses on things that require its attention in a given moment. If you are crossing a busy street, your brain knows to focus on the moving cars and not the birds in the tree on the other side.

It also knows how to fill in the blanks. A big truck may have stopped to let you cross, but your brain knows there might be a car on the other side of the truck it can't see.

These instincts are of course useful—they just don't know when to stop. Your mind is constantly making its own decisions on what it focuses on and what it puts into your visual blind spots. It's up to you to train your brain to see more.

Here's an example: Look at the image below and tell yourself what you see behind the bars:

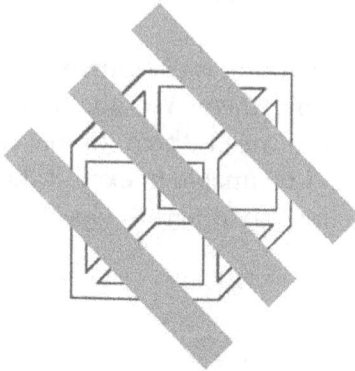

Your brain probably told you, "It's a cube. I've seen plenty of cubes before. It might have three bars in front of it, but it is a cube."

In fact, the only visual representation of a cube being sent to your brain is this:

The pieces are difficult to perceive as a cube when they are seen on their own. Our brain uses its previous knowledge of a cube to fill in the blanks behind the obstructing bars.

You were able to perceive a cube in the first image because you had "visual bias" of what a whole cube looks like and used that knowledge to fill in the missing pieces.

As Tracy writes, "Learning is essentially about updating our biases, not eliminating them. We always need them to get started, but we also need them to be open to change, otherwise we would be unable to exploit the new vistas that our advancing technology opens to view."

Example: ColaLife

Simon Berry was frustrated that people were able to buy a bottle of Coke in developing nations more easily than they were able to obtain essential medicines. He had a dream to make medicine as easy to obtain in those countries as it was to get a Coke.

"The dream," reported Forbes Magazine, "transpired into using Coca-Cola's distribution networks to deliver affordable medicines for childhood diseases to remote rural communities where medical care was scarce but Coca-Cola was not."

Within Coke's vast global supply network, Berry saw a sliver of space in one part of the operation and realized it contained the extra ability he needed. It was the room between Coca-Cola bottles in crates. He looked at the space, just a few inches high and wide, and thought:

"This could be where medicines ship with the soda."

He shared his observation online and quickly built a following. A network of supporters crowdsourced the design and manufacturing of the "Kit Yamayo," or "Kit of Life," to prevent children dying of diarrhea.

The kit consists of a package of oral re-hydration solutions, zinc soap, and educational materials, all contained inside a custom-designed wedge pack.

ColaLife trialed its kits in Zambia where Coke is abundant but one in four children die of diarrhea each year. After using the empty space in Coke crates as its distribution vehicle for one year, the kits reached almost 45 percent of the children who needed them.

In 2013 the United Nations General Assembly labeled the kit as one of the top ten breakthrough innovations in mother and child health care that could save lives.

Sometimes all it takes is the ability to see opportunity in a few inches of empty space to make a dent in the universe.

Worksheet: Using A Cube

Let's take another look at the cube.

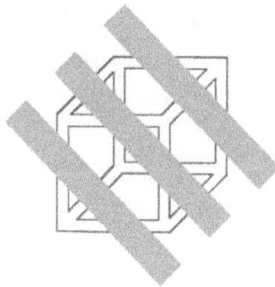

Look at the image again and think or sketch **something you could make with the cube behind the bars**:

Chances are, you thought about using the cube as an object; maybe as the foundation for something or as a piece of a larger construction.

But remember, what you really have to work with are just pieces:

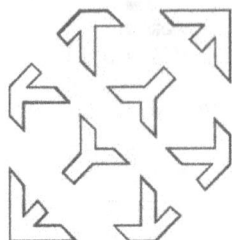

It's the same cube your eyes perceived before, but its capabilities are considerably greater when you accurately see it as a collection of pieces. Now try again:

What can you make using the cube?

The potential of utilizing an object in new ways is always greater when you see what is actually present instead of what your brain perceives.

STEP 3: USE NEW WORDS

Asked to name a material that comes from a tree, most people would say, "a piece of wood."

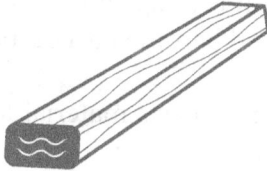

It's an adequate name for the material, but "a piece of wood" is its identity for only a moment in time:

- It was once a seed, then a sapling, then a tree.

- Once the tree it was cut down, it became a log.

- The log was milled and became a piece of wood.

- The wood will become a table, a chair, part of a house, or something else.

- In time, it will degrade and return to the earth and the process will begin again.

"A piece of wood" is a temporary identity, forever in a state of flux. In fact, everything is in a temporary state between its current reality and its future state.

In his book *Zen Keys*, Thich Nhat Hanh writes, "All phenomena [physical, psychological, and physiological] are devoid of a permanent identity."

"If they were not impermanent, how could a grain of corn grow into an ear of corn? How could your little girl grow up into a beautiful young lady? Things are possible only when they are devoid of a fixed identity."

Whatever is described with a "This is" label only exists as that identity for that moment.

If you pick up a leaf and say, "This is a leaf," you're not going to be able to say the same thing about that leaf next year when it has decomposed and become part of the forest floor.

When your daughter requests material for her pottery class, you can hand her some and say:

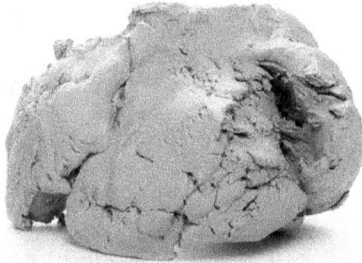

"This is a lump of clay."

But when she proudly shows you what she made...

You're in a lot of trouble if you say the same thing.

Understanding that things do not exist in a fixed state is the gateway to discovering more fluid, agile, and meaningful uses for everything. It can be a mental stretch at first to let go of fixed identities. Deep inside we like to have as much certainty in our world as possible.

"Most aspects of our culture currently lead us to try to reduce uncertainty," says Langer (of the rubber band study). "We learn so that we will know what things are. Instead, we should consider exploiting the power of uncertainty so that we can learn what things can become."

You will have more assets to work with—and the ability to work in a more future-positive way—when you realize all things are themselves part of a larger journey, a larger process, a larger timeline.

Removing absolute definitions from things removes the limitations of their current form.

Altering the words we use in relation to things is one of the best tools we have to generate new thinking and uses for existing assets. We have the freedom to use any word we want to describe anything.

In fact, researchers have found that this ability comes pre-installed in us. Our brains are designed to separate the mental process of seeing something from the act of understanding it.

In the 1970s Elizabeth K. Warrington and Angela M. Taylor performed a study on patients who had damage to cognitive areas of the brain but no damage to their visual pathways.

As American Scientist[28] reports on the study, "It transpired that the part of the brain that's active when we identify the three-dimensional shape of an object (say, a cylindrical white item on the desk) is different from the area involved in knowing its purpose or name (a coffee cup that holds your next sip)."

Every time you encounter an object, material, or other asset, your brain literally gives you space to work with between visual recognition of the object and your understanding of what you see.

Use that ability to change your perception of objects and their potential. If you've ever used a coffee cup to hold pens or kept a bag of chips shut with a clothespin, you've already tapped into the potential that exists between an object's visual identity and your understanding of its function.

Let's try a quick experiment to explore this.

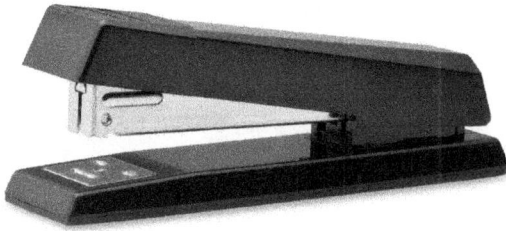

Look at the image above and tell yourself the device is called a joiner.

You learned that it is called a stapler because it staples pages together, but it also joins pages together. Did it get its name because it uses staples?

It might seem like trivial wordplay, but for the first time you actually thought about a stapler: what it does, what its name is, and why it has that name.

Calling it by a different name activated synapses in your brain that were just kicking back in ho-hum routine every other time you saw a stapler.

The language we use when we introduce ourselves—and others—to things make a big difference.

"We don't just use language to communicate with others, we use it to think to ourselves," writes Dr. David Ludden in *How Language Shapes Our World*.[29] "We see the world according to the framework our language imposes on us."

Look at the following objects and read the words below each one:

This could be a coffee cup.

This could be a table.

This could be a coat rack.

When you saw a familiar object at the same time you read "This could..." something very important was happening—your brain was working harder than usual.

The disconnect between your visual perception of a known object and another part of your brain registering the conditional phrase "This could..." sparked new mental processes.

Looking at things with "This is" in mind gives your brain no reason to get the neurons ready for to make new connections. "This is" is an absolute term, and whatever comes next, those words already told your brain it was in familiar territory so it can just relax and keep working on what you'll order for lunch.

Your Brain on Absolute Phrases

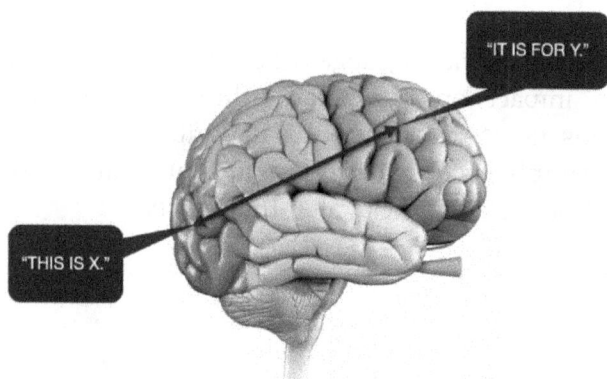

However, when your brain sees a familiar object and processes the words "This could..." in relation to that object, things change. The words tell your brain a conditional moment is present, and it begins preparing to make new connections.

Your Brain on Conditional Phrases

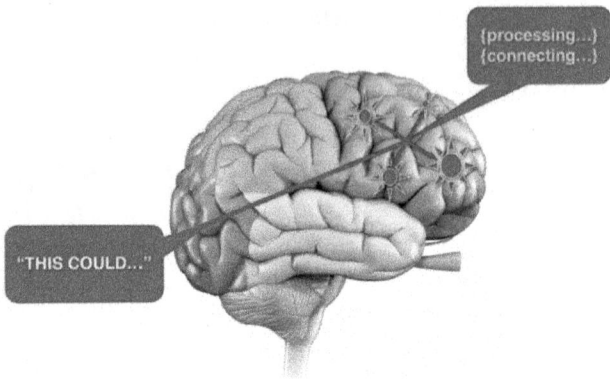

The conditional phrase signaled that options and possibilities were coming and you needed to get ready for some heavier-than-usual processing. It began to make new synaptic connections between the object and the creative and analytical areas of your brain.

Minor tweaks in the language we use to describe things have a huge impact on our relationship to everything that surrounds us. As Joel N. Shurkin writes in LiveScience[30], "Vision simply isn't as objective a view of reality as we think it is. Just saying a word can alter that reality."

Example: Opod Tube House

Hong Kong suffers from an acute shortage of affordable housing options.

Those who can afford it pay well over $2,000 a month for a tiny one-bedroom apartment, while the average household needs to spend 19 years' worth of income to purchase an apartment.[31]

With development limited by the city's island constraints, local firm James Law Cybertecture realized that new housing options would require new thinking about how existing urban assets could be used. Specifically, the firm looked at large water infrastructure pipes and thought:

"This could be affordable housing."

The firm's "Opod Tube House" concept "is an experimental, low-cost, micro-housing unit to ease Hong Kong's affordable housing problems."

"Constructed out of low-cost and readily available 2.5-meter diameter concrete water pipe, the design utilizes the strong concrete structure to house a micro-living apartment for one/two persons with fully kitted out living, cooking, and bathroom spaces inside 100 square feet."

The dimensions may seem small to some, but as more than 200,000 Hong Kong residents live in sub-divided apartments that average 130 square feet before being divided, and thousands more live in 20-square-foot "coffin homes," Opod Tube Houses are attractive alternatives.

The firm estimates that each OPod Tube House can be built for approximately $15,000 and rented out for about $400 a month. Opod Tube House's small footprint allows one or more to fit in vacant lots or unused spaces between buildings for flexible housing solutions.

The units can also be stacked to become a multi-unit modular housing complex for a fraction of traditional housing development costs.

Worksheet: This Could…

Let's start forming some new synaptic connections in your brain. Use "This could…" to describe the objects below to give them a new use or identity.

STEP 4: CONSIDER COMPONENTS

While you were contemplating new uses and identities for the objects, you were doing something else at the same time: you were overcoming your "functional fixedness."

The term was coined by Psychologist Karl Duncker in 1945 to describe a "mental block against using an object in a new way that is required to solve a problem."

To explore this condition Duncker created an experiment in which he presented one group of participants with a candle, a box of thumbtacks, and a book of matches.

Participants were then told to attach the lit candle to the wall in a way that would prevent wax from dripping onto the table below. Most tried attaching the candle directly to the wall with the tacks (fail) or using melted wax to glue the candle to the wall (fail).

Duncker observed that the majority of participants were "fixated" with the box's function as a container for tacks and could not imagine it performing another task.

He then gave a second group of participants the same materials, with one slight change: the tacks were removed from the box and placed beside it.

With the tacks and the box presented as separate entities, participants more easily understood that the box could have other functions.

The majority of participants in the second group placed the candle in the box, then tacked the box to the wall (for the win).

The experiment inspired a later study to see if language alone could overcome perceived limitations of an object.

In 1980 psychologists E. Tory Higgins and William M. Chaires replicated the candle experiment with a linguistic twist[32]— when participants were issued the experiment materials, the boxes of tacks were introduced with a one-word alteration.

The first group was given the box of tacks with the label:

"A Box **of** Tacks."

The second group was given an identical box of tacks with the label:

"A Box **and** Tacks."

In the group that was given "a box *of* tacks," **20 percent** of participants used the box to hold the candle.

In the group that was given "a box *and* tacks," **80 percent** of participants used the box to hold the candle.

The experiment mirrored Duncker's findings—when participants were given a box "of" tacks they registered it as a single entity, and few were able to separate container and contents as two separate assets.

Changing just one word—a box "and" tacks—allowed participants to free themselves from fixed notions of the box's function and realize that each asset had separate capabilities and possibilities for use.

Contents and Components

We often lock objects into linear equations of *"This is X, and it is for Y."* One example is how people perceive a takeout coffee cup.

Most would look at it and say, "This is a coffee cup, and it is for drinking coffee outside of the cafe." But if we examine it more thoroughly, we see that the coffee cup is actually a combination of:

- The stirrer
- The lid
- The paper cup
- The cardboard holder
- The coffee (and its heat, liquid capabilities, cooling dynamics)

Identifying an object by its components instead of as a singular object increases awareness of its capabilities.

Example: Bus Stop Light Therapy

Umeå, Sweden, sits 300 miles north of Stockholm. During the winter months, residents receive very little sunlight. "If," one resident notes, "the sun shines at all."

Lack of natural light for long periods of time can have a serious impact on the mental health of individuals and the wellbeing of the city as a whole. The city's energy company, Umeå Energi, wanted to do something to help battle the seasonal depression caused by the lack of natural light.

The company identified a city asset with the capacity to do more: bus shelters. When the structures were examined in terms of their components, several options for new use were revealed.

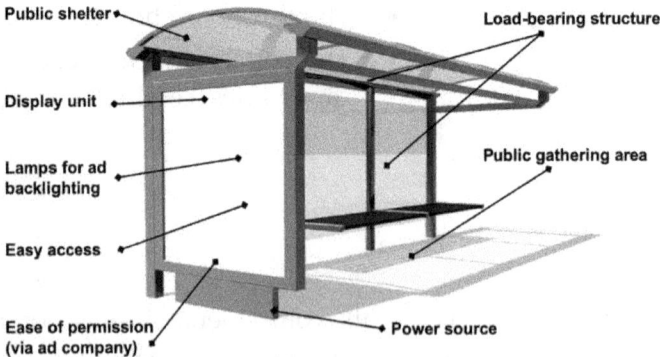

Public shelter
Load-bearing structure
Display unit
Lamps for ad backlighting
Public gathering area
Easy access
Ease of permission (via ad company)
Power source

Umeå Energi focused on the capabilities of the advertising unit and the light bulbs in contained to back-light ads.

The advertising lights in 30 of the city's bus stops were replaced with light therapy bulbs that emit the equivalent of natural sunlight. A clear sheet was then placed in each advertising frame to allow the light to shine through.

The new "Ljusterapi" (Light Therapy) bus stops allow commuters to spend a few minutes facing the therapeutic lights while waiting for the bus to soak up the benefits of the sun they miss during the winter.

Bus riders described feeling happier and more positive after spending time in the light therapy bus stops. After the light therapy bulbs were installed bus use in the city doubled.

Worksheet: Content and Components

Identify one or more pieces of content (objects, devices, materials) around you right now. Write the name(s) below then describe it using "and" to separate the thing into its parts. For example:

- A pen might be "a plastic tube *and* stylus *and* ink"
- A light could be "a socket *and* power *and* lightbulb"

The more times you can use "and" to describe it, the better.

Original Object:

Can be described as:

and   *and*

Original Object:

Can be described as:

and   *and*

By separating something into its parts, you reveal its underlying resources and their extra abilities.

STEP 5: CREATE NEW CONTEXTS

Creating new contexts of use for existing content is the axis of opportunity for the future. Because while everything is content, not all content is used in the best possible context.

The light therapy bus stop illustrates content vs. context:

Content   *Context*

Imagine if we explored all existing assets, materials, resources, *everything*, with deliberate, intentional pursuit of improving its context of use—if everything was seen as content and its components were considered tools to meet new needs.

It is a necessary shift in thinking about existing assets. For while the world is near critical density in terms of content, we lack a critical analysis if that content is being used in the best context.

Nature offers some exceptional examples of finding new contexts of use for existing content.

Japanese crows used to drop walnuts onto rocks from high above to crack them open. As the crows' rock habitats were replaced by buildings and streets, they realized the streets could be used in a different context to crack open nuts.

Today it is common to see crows with walnuts in their mouths perched over pedestrian crossings. They drop the nuts onto the crossing below, let the car tires crack them open, and wait for the crossing signal to sound before retrieving them. They know the crossing signal sound means the cars are going to stop, so that's the moment to safely get their food.

In New York City, the RFK Triborough Bridge is a piece of content that takes cars and people across the water, as bridges are supposed to do. But Red-Tailed Hawks see it in a different context.

The bridge's overhang provides excellent shelter for the hawks and its large cable housings are a better foundation for their weighty nests better than most tree branches. And being New York, it's all about location.

A nest under the lip of the bridge overlooks fish-filled waters and cement crevices where rodents and pigeons gather. From a hawk's point of view it's like living in a loft with a Whole Foods on the floor below.

Scientists refer to the abilities of animals to adapt to and utilize new environments in new contexts as "rapid evolution." We need to embark on our own rapid evolution to use our assets in better contexts.

The birds are able to create new contexts of use because they do not have a fixed notion of how specific pieces of content are *supposed* to be used—they simply use them in a context that meets their needs. Our situation is not that different, but we are still tied to fixed perceptions of use for the content that form our cities and our lives.

We must adapt to a new truth: we have a finite amount of content available to us. It is the context of how we use our content that is the limitless resource we have to work with.

Example: Linha Jose

While shopping in the street markets of Sao Paulo, Brazilian designer Mauricio Arruda saw the potential to use the market's plastic crates in a new context.

The crates are used to carry produce and goods from wholesalers to vendor stalls. Customers who buy large quantities of items take full crates home, shift the goods to another container, then discard the plastic crates.

As Arruda says on his website, he contemplated a new context for the crates in terms of "the entire product life, trying to lessen material and energy waste, environmental impact, and worrying about the socio-economic and cultural aspects of its use." Arruda realized:

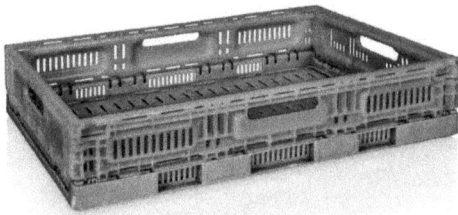

"This could be used in furniture."

His Linha Jose line of furniture incorporates the plastic crates and extends their function beyond use in the market.

Linha Jose, says Arruda, "Enables users to store and transport objects, toys, food, clothes, books, bottles, or anything else inside and outside the home."

"Shopping, for example, can be transported between the market and home, eliminating the use of plastic bags. Furthermore, the boxes can be rearranged depending on the user's needs."

Worksheet: Creating New Contexts

What extra abilities exist in the pieces of content that make up your surroundings, or the processes used by you or your company?

Object/Process:

Components:

Qualities or Capabilities:

- Can its function be improved or upgraded?
- Can it host a "plug-in" structure or service?
- Can it be re-imagined for a different use?

What else could it do?

What else could it be?

STEP 6: SHIFT SKILLS

Of all assets with potential for new use, skills are among the most dynamic. They are internal resources able to be employed in new ways without relying on additional material resources.

The full potential of a skill, however, is never realized when it is locked within a set discipline.

I once saw a dance film that made such an impression, I sought out the producer after its screening. I asked what his secret was to capturing human movement so fluidly and beautifully on film.

"I only hire NFL cameramen to shoot my films," was his reply. I chuckled cynically to call his bluff. There was no bluff.

"Their entire career is spent tracking individuals who move quickly and unpredictably," he explained. "The skills they develop over the years, the instincts they hone—play after play, game after game—puts them in an entirely different league when it comes to capturing movement."

That exchange always comes to mind when I think the power of "cross-pollinating" skills across disciplines.

The ability for the producer to look at the skills of NFL cameramen and think, "This could be used to capture the movement of dancers on screen," is a prime example of using skills in new contexts for exceptional results. History has plenty of examples of this.

When the Terracotta Army was discovered in 1974 researchers found similarities between the legs of the army figures and the water drainpipes created during the same period. As the History Channel reported:

"The restoration process revealed how the figures originally had been made ... Craftsmen who knew how to make terracotta drainage pipes applied their skill to create the figures using molds and an assembly line production system of body parts. Once the figures were assembled, distinctive surface features were applied with clay."

Different skills offer new perspectives, backgrounds, and experiences for fresh solutions when assigned to a new field.

Specialized skill sets too often remain as closed loops of knowledge and execution. Everyone loses when this is the case. All it takes is to step back from the linear "this skill is for this task," and think of the skill set as content ready for use in a new context.

Example: Pandemic Skill Shifts

Thousands of employees from the travel and hospitality industry were fired or furloughed during the pandemic.

Most countries saw these individuals as another subset of the unemployed. Sweden saw them as skilled resources with abilities to meet pressing needs of the time.

Airline Crews and Hotel Employees

Some cabin crew members from Scandinavia's SAS Airlines signed up to train at Sophiahemmet University, a nursing school and private hospital.

University president Johanna Adami said the crews' existing skills made them well-suited for helping during the pandemic. "They are trained in first aid, the most common diseases, and also safety and how to care for people."[33]

In addition to being trained in how to deal with medical emergencies onboard, they are trained to handle tense moments such as dealing with unruly passengers—all skills that can help during stressful situations in hospitals.

"We're really good at being around people and taking care of people," says flight attendant Mathilda Malm, who was part of the training program. "We're always prepared for every situation and we handle it in a calm way."[34]

Building on its success with airline employees, Stockholm's "Skill Shift Initiative," set up by recruitment agency Novare, SAS, and the Wallenberg Foundations, gave furloughed hotel employees a chance to apply their skills in new ways.

Staff from Stockholm's Grand Hotel augmented their hospitality skills with specialized training to care for the elderly, then assisted in local nursing homes.

Stockholm mayor Anna Konig Jerlmyr told the AP that she saw transferring the skills of airline staff and hotel workers as "a way of optimizing our resources" to meet the city's urgent needs.

Costume Makers

The entertainment industry was another field brought to a halt by the pandemic. Theaters went dark, concerts were cancelled, and television and film productions were stopped.

When the industry's skills weren't needed on the set or stage, they used them to help, as one person put it, "Real-life superheroes, unlike the fictional ones we're used to working with."

In the UK, costume designers from the TV series "His Dark Materials" put their skills to work creating scrubs for essential medical personnel.

Costume designer Caroline McCall told BBC News the idea began when she and other show staff became aware that there were "many and varied talents within the film industry that would not be in use at this time," and could be put to use to help others.

"In our jobs," says costume supervisor Dulcie Scott, "we're used to hitting the ground running, looking around and going, 'Right, what can I do?' Working as a team, problem solving, and having to think on your feet."

Dulcie took the lead to form a network of costume designers and stitchers dubbed "Helping Dress Medics." She set up a GoFundMe page to solicit donations for the materials needed, and within a couple weeks received 10 times the requested amount. The TV show's buyer stepped in to help source the fabric and materials, while the publicity crew pitched in to promote the initiative.

As word spread through the industry, other volunteers came forward creating a who's who list of the British costume design community, with designers from "Batman," "Guardians of the Galaxy," "Cinderella," and the English National Opera joining the effort.

"Our roll call is embarrassingly brilliant," Scott told CNN. "I think the film industry internationally takes pride in being able to adapt, move with speed, go as required, see a problem and sort it."

The expanded team, all working from home, produced over 10,000 scrubs for a range of hospices, hospitals, clinics, and elderly people's homes throughout the UK.

Worksheet: Shift Your Skills

What skills, training, and experience do you have?

When have you found yourself employing your personal skills or expertise outside of your own discipline?

How could you apply your skills in different contexts to help others or to meet others' needs?

SECTION THREE

BUILDING RESILIENCE

"Give me six hours to chop down a tree,
and I will spend the first four sharpening the axe."
- Abraham Lincoln

The steps you've just gone through have increased your internal resources, started forming new connections in your brain, increased your resourcefulness, and built up your resilience. Every time you use them, you'll keep building new connections and resources.

Why is this important? In the short term, looking at things differently and creating new associations between an asset's current state and what it *could be* forms new synaptic connections in our brains.

Do it enough and it begins to change how you think, allowing new opportunities to present themselves more frequently in your career and daily life.

In the long term, these skills do something else tremendously important. They prepare you for future uncertainty. Because let's face it—the only thing certain about the future is that it is uncertain.

We can surround ourselves with supplies needed to sustain our basic needs during uncertain times, but it is our internal resources of agility and resilience that will actually get us through periods of uncertainty.

In the spring of 2020, nations, businesses, communities, and individuals were planning for the coming year. Then the Covid-19 pandemic struck, upending almost every plan for the foreseeable future and bringing normal life to a halt. Millions felt vulnerable as the Coronavirus spread, shattering the predictabilities of daily life, social norms, and economics.

What quickly became apparent was those who approached difficulties with an agile approach—those who were able to look at existing resources conditionally and think, "This could..." were able to respond to rapidly changing circumstances quickly and resourcefully.

Conditional thinking is a powerful tool to counter the vulnerability people feel when they are not prepared for a situation. As our skill sets grow and our internal resources increase, so do the tools and abilities to face uncertainty.

The resourcefulness gained from viewing things with "This could..." in mind provides more abilities and preparedness to counter vulnerability.

The attributes built in this book and honed through resourceful practice and conditional thinking increases your sustainable attributes—not only in terms of consumption and waste reduction, but in your ability to sustain yourself during uncertain times.

I refer to the skills and abilities to solve unexpected problems using available resources as "sustainable attributes."

Sustainable Attributes

Sustainable attributes are the inner qualities conditional thinking buildings within us. They are attributes that will see us through to the other side of tough times and help us emerge with greater confidence and ability.

The sustainable attributes that help deal with uncertainty are:

Agility

Needs change more quickly than physical resources are able to increase. Agility provides an ability to respond to quickly changing needs by using available assets in new ways.

Ability

Being fully aware of your existing resources and their components and capabilities gives you a resource-aware perspective to quickly address shortcomings without depending on additional external resources.

Resilience

By reducing dependence on external resources, an agile ecosystem of available resources to provide solutions for existing needs can be created at any scale.

Resourcefulness

The ability to do more with what you have turns limited resources into tools for flexible solutions, greater self-sufficiency, and empowerment.

The steps you've gone through in this book build each of these essential attributes to help navigate uncertain times.

At the heart of it all is conditional thinking—the ability to face the current situation in a flexible manner by looking at things in a fluid context and realizing there is always a path forward.

DO WHAT YOU CAN

"You'll never catch me bragging about goals,
but I'll talk all you want about my assists."
- Wayne Gretzky

You've now got the tools to begin changing things and respond dynamically to new needs. The most important advice I can offer now is to not get hung up on goals.

Looking at something—an object, a system, a budget—with "This could…" in mind is intention without a goal. It is about movement forward—a pivot towards a new reality. "This could…" is about providing the assist for the larger victory.

Wayne Gretzky holds the record for most goals scored in the NHL with 1,016 goals. He also holds the record for most assists with 2,223 passes to other players that led to goals.

There is a lesson in comparing the numbers: 2,223 > 1,106. Assisting others leads to more goals than you can score on your own.

One night Michael Jordan scored a record 69 points in a play-off game for the Chicago Bulls. His rookie teammate Stacey King scored just one point in the same game from a free throw.

After the game a reporter interviewed King. He said:

"I'll always remember this as the night Michael and I combined to score 70 points."

Imagine being Stacey King during the game as Jordan sinks shot after shot, knowing that there's no way your efforts can match such a performance. But when King was fouled and went to the line to shoot his free throw, his perspective was firmly in place: "This is what I can do right now to be part of the win."

The new perspectives and capabilities you've acquired in this book will most likely appear in a familiar form—intuition. Your intuition will spark more frequently now, often during moments or situations you coasted through previously.

Let that intuition be your driver to do what you can. To provide the assist for a goal or score the single point that goes on the board as being part of the victory. As Theodore Roosevelt's said, "Do what you can, with what you've got, where you are."

Use your intuition to make your business, your life, and your place in the world a better and more resourceful place. Look at what you have and think, "This could..." be something different; something better.

Don't get stuck on achieving a specific goal or worrying if the rest of the world is doing its part. Just what you can. Score your point to add to the others being scored. Just be sure to take a shot, because as Gretzky also said, "You miss 100 percent of the shots you don't take."

FIX SOMETHING

Did you hear that snapping sound? That's you breaking the tape at the finish line. You've reached the end of the book.

This is usually where the summary would go, but summaries bring things to a close. That's not what is going to happen here. Instead, I'm going to leave you with a task:

fix something.

I'm not talking about repairing something to its previous state. Don't get me wrong—it's an important thing to keep things from being discarded, and one that should be constantly practiced and encouraged.

At the same time, returning something to its original state only brings it back to where it started.

In the same moment something breaks, opportunity is created. In the moment of repair, two paths present themselves: fix it like it was or fix it better. The first option is an act of restoration. The second is one of transformation.

Fix it Better

When programmers go into code to fix bugs, they often find opportunities to fix other functions of the code.

The same can occur while repairing something. Think of repair in terms of versioning. You could discard it and buy the latest version, or you could use the moment of repair to upgrade its capabilities to a new version yourself.

The starting point for all options is the same—something is broken, and the decision is made to open it up and see what went wrong. The defective part, element, unit, etc., is identified. Now questions can be asked—is there a better version of the defective part available?

By putting an improved part in its place, will it become more efficient, faster, fun? Or, reflecting back on the power of components, take a look at everything *else* that makes up the unit you've taken apart. Is this the moment to make it do something entirely different?

This leads to the most impactful act of fixing things—fixing the content's context.

Fix the Context of Content

Look beyond your personal objects for ways to improve the world. Look at *all* available resources—your skills, your city's physical assets, your company's processes and products—and ask yourself:

"Is this content being used in the best possible context? Is it being used to its full capacity? Is it meeting a need?"

If the answer to any of these questions is no, then that content needs to be fixed.

Keep parking garages and other examples in mind. Were those pieces of content being used in their best possible context? When hospitals ran out of room to process and treat patients, they didn't need adequate parking. Their parking garages were content that was not being used in its best possible content, so they were fixed to do so.

Our collective responsibility extends beyond our actions as consumers. We have a responsibility to ensure our resources—physical, financial, natural, material, and all others—are used in the most responsible way possible.

If the resources we have—our content—do not meet current and future needs, it is our responsibility to change the context of use and fix them so they do.

Creating new contexts of use for existing content is scalable and brings benefits at any level of engagement.

You don't need to transform a parking garage or a bus stop—finding a new context of use for any content you would otherwise discard is a vitally important motion forward towards a better world.

You now have the tools to re-imagine any piece of content and its components and ensure they are used in the best possible context. If they aren't—fix them.

Every moment you look at something that could serve another purpose or be improved to meet a new need you are at a fulcrum point between past and future.

You have a material, object, or resource from the past. You are the catalyst to move it to a future state. It's a powerful place to find yourself.

"The present moment contains past and future. The secret of transformation is in the way we handle this very moment."

- Thich Nhat Hanh

ABOUT THE AUTHOR

Scott Burnham, FRSA, is an author and strategist behind dozens of initiatives worldwide that have helped companies, cities, and institutions do more with the assets they already have.

He created Reprogramming the City, a global initiative encouraging cities to be more resilient by repurposing and reimagining the use of existing urban assets, and has curated over 30 exhibitions in eight nations exploring new ideas for design, resourcefulness, and innovation.

Burnham has addressed The World Bank, The World Urban Development Congress, and many other organizations on resilient design strategies and increasing creative capital in cities. He is the author of *Reprogramming the City*, the toolkit *How to Reprogram the City*, *NatureStructure*, *Design Hacking*, *Urban Play*, and *Trust Design*, and contributes to numerous publications ranging from The Guardian to Architizer.

In recognition of his work, Burnham was made a Fellow of the Royal Society for Arts, Manufacturers and Commerce in London in 2009.

For more information, visit **scottburnham.com**

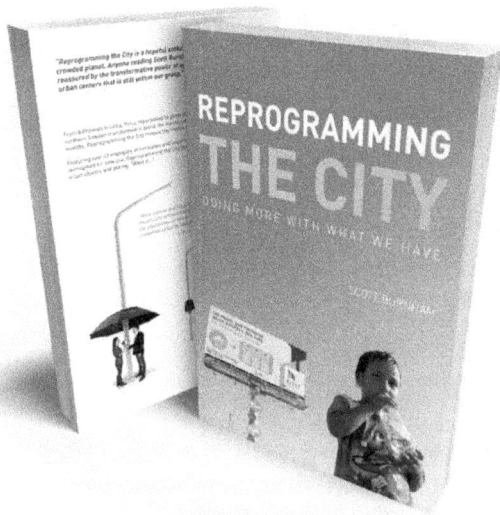

If you are interested in doing more with what already exists in our cities the Reprogramming the City book is for you!

Featuring 44 projects from 17 countries, it is a collection of ideas to make cities more resilient by using existing urban objects in new ways.

"A hopeful anthology of solutions for our hot, crowded planet. Anyone reading Scott Burnham's essential book will emerge reassured by the transformative power of creativity."

— *Renée Loth, AchitectureBoston magazine*

Available at:

www.reprogrammingthecity.com

CREDITS AND CITATIONS

[1] https://brainly.com/question/12043780

[2] Zittel, W. (2012) "Feasible Future for the Common Good: Energy Transition Paths in a Period of Increasing Resource Scarcities", *Progress Report 1: Assessment of Fossil Fuels Availability [Task 2a] and of Key Metals Availability [Task 2b]* (Sustainable Europe Research Institute, Vienna)

[3] https://www.epa.gov/facts-and-figures-about-materials-waste-and-recycling/national-overview-facts-and-figures-materials

[4] https://covid19.nlc.org/wp-content/uploads/2020/06/What-Covid-19-Means-For-City-Finances_Report-Final.pdf

[5] https://apnews.com/article/health-international-news-business-ursula-von-der-leyen-virus-outbreak-cae852fcdb1bded4d8740e785419871a

[6] Creating A Culture Of Creativity, L. A. Vint; International Design Conference - Design 2006

[7] https://hbr.org/2017/03/our-brains-love-new-stuff-and-its-killing-the-planet

[8] https://www.topspeed.com/cars/bmw/2020-bmw-1-series-ar163870.html

[9] https://www.goodreads.com/en/book/show/40180024-cr-ft

[10] https://www.huffpost.com/entry/shopping-on-thanksgiving_b_4310109

[11] Page 7, "Fewer, Better Things," Glenn Adamson

[12] https://www.axios.com/the-future-of-parking-garages-98ae0851-885f-4ba8-a910-255c751cc38c.html

[13] https://www.popularmechanics.com/technology/gadgets/a21841/nike-waffle-iron/

[14] https://www.sciencedirect.com/science/article/abs/pii/105381009290066J

[15] https://www.scientificamerican.com/article/london-taxi-memory/

[16] https://georgia.growingamerica.com/features/2018/02/farmer-mod-1800s-barbed-wire-phone-line

[17] http://gizmodo.com/barbed-wire-fences-were-an-early-diy-telephone-network-1493157700

[18] George Land and Beth Jarman, Breaking Point and Beyond. San Francisco: HarperBusiness, 1993

[19] https://hbr.org/2016/03/learning-to-learn

[20] https://www.nytimes.com/2018/12/07/opinion/sunday/end-the-innovation-obsession.html

[21] https://www.mensjournal.com/health-fitness/how-distilleries-now-making-hand-sanitizer/

[22] https://www.nytimes.com/2016/06/19/opinion/sunday/think-less-think-better.html

[23] https://www.popularmechanics.com/science/energy/g600/6-ways-to-harness-wasted-transit-energy/?slide=3

[24] http://mithya.prasadkaipa.com/learning/howunlearn.html

[25] https://www.americanscientist.org/article/learning-to-see

[26] Source: Drew T, Võ ML-H, Wolfe JM. The Invisible Gorilla Strikes Again: Sustained Inattentional Blindness in Expert Observers. Psychological Science. 2013.

[27] https://www.medicaldaily.com/inattentional-blindess-why-83-radiologists-couldnt-see-gorilla-247871

[28] https://www.americanscientist.org/article/learning-to-see

[29] https://www.psychologytoday.com/us/blog/talking-apes/201509/how-language-shapes-our-world

[30] https://www.livescience.com/38870-hearing-a-word-can-help-you-see-the-invisible.html

[31] https://www.theguardian.com/cities/2019/jul/12/are-artificial-islands-the-answer-to-hong-kongs-housing-crisis

[32] www.sciencedirect.com/science/article/abs/pii/002210318090027X?via%3Dihub

[33] https://www.thelocal.se/20200411/furloughed-staff-in-sweden-retrain-to-help-hospitals

[34] https://www.clickorlando.com/business/2020/04/01/reporting-for-duty-airline-crew-sign-up-to-help-hospitals/